Tea Parties for DADS

A Crash Course in Daughters for New Fathers

Jenna McCarthy

SASQUATCH BOOKS
SEATTLE

Printed in Canada
Published by Sasquatch Books
Distributed by PGW/Perseus
15 14 13 12 11 10   10 9 8 7 6 5 4 3 2 1

Cover and interior design: Rosebud Eustace
Cover and interior illustrations: Sasha Barr

Library of Congress Cataloging-in-Publication Data

McCarthy, Jenna.
 Tea parties for dads : a crash course in daughters for new fathers / Jenna McCarthy.
   p. cm.
  ISBN 978-1-57061-623-5
 1. Fatherhood--Humor. 2. Clothing and dress--Humor. 3. Fathers and daughters--Humor. I. Title.
  PN6231.F37M39 2010
  818'.607--dc22
                    2009039489

Sasquatch Books
119 South Main Street, Suite 400
Seattle, WA 98104
(206) 467-4300
www.sasquatchbooks.com
custserv@sasquatchbooks.com

Contents

Introduction

You may be a snappy dresser and know your way around a wok, but at the end of the day, you're a guy. As such, you probably are pretty well-versed—or at least, more proficient than your parenting partner—on the topics of sports, beer, excavators, and electronics. You can bait a hook, handcraft a homemade bottle rocket, and whip together the world's coolest tree fort during halftime intermission. Car's making a funny noise? You might even be known to stick your head under the hood before calling a mechanic. Now here you are, not just having a baby (which is daunting in and of itself), you're having a *daughter*.

Gulp.

No matter how in touch with your feminine side you might be, there is bound to come a time when you are downright dumbfounded by your little girl's fascination with fairies or her obsession with all things sparkly. Your pint-size princess may barely be fluent in the English language the first time she asks you to paint her tiny toenails, and trust us, she'll expect you to know the critical difference between a pigtail and a ponytail when she bequeaths the hairdresser hat upon you.

Before you break out in a cold sweat, rest assured that—with your helpful guidance and enthusiasm— she's also likely to love digging for worms, pounding on pretend nails with her plastic hammer, and shooting hoops with you in the driveway for hours on end. She may one day beg you to go scat-tracking with her on the local trails or teach *you* how to change a truck tire.

But until that day comes, think of this book as your guide to all things girly. It will help you understand why in your daughter's eyes, there's really only one color in the world (pink), teach you to fashion her hair into an array of acceptable styles, and reveal the secret reasons why mermaids and magic wands are so utterly irresistible to her.

The good news is you'll already be your daughter's hero just by virtue of being her dad. So go ahead and take her to the racetrack and teach her to distinguish a cylinder from a crankshaft. Impress her with your manly tie-tying skills and astound her with your feats of strength, like holding her high above your head with one hand. But do it after you French braid her hair or enjoy a tea party with her posse of tutu-clad teddy bears and your status will go from hero to superhero *just like that*.

Think PINK!

"I have a surprise for you," you might sing-song one day in the not-too-distant future.

"Is it pink?" she'll ask, squinting at you.

"It's squirmy!" you'll offer mysteriously, eyebrows raised.

"Is it pink?" she'll demand, undaunted.

"It's a lizard!" you'll say proudly.

"Is it *pink*?"

"Well, no, not exactly . . . " you'll stammer, the thought bubble over your head reading, "What gives?"

Here's the thing with little girls and the invariably preferred hue: pink is not just a color—it's a way of life. It's synonymous with girly, feminine, and fancy. It's *pretty*. (Remember, they didn't name the movie *Pretty in Puce*.) From the palest pastel blush to the boldest rose to blinding neon fuchsia, if it doesn't fall on the pinkalicious spectrum, she may very well veto it on principle.

Kitchen tip

Forget green-eggs-and-ham, Dad. Food tastes best when it's pink! Add a few drops of red food coloring to her applesauce, cottage cheese, or oatmeal and watch her lick the bowl clean. At snack time, introduce her to strawberry milk and really blow her mind!

Back in the day (your day, to be precise), pink was for Barbies and baby blankets—and of course, Pepto-Bismol. Today, if they make it, they make it in pink. Soccer and tennis balls, bicycles and skateboards, Band-Aids, and even braces all can be procured in the winning tint. Don't try to fight it, Dad—it's hardwired into her. Instead, score major papa-points by jumping on board the bubblegum bandwagon. Paint her bedroom in shades of raspberry and rose. Don't try to convince her she'll hit a standard-issue *yellow* tennis ball harder and farther than the magenta model her little heart adores. Tell her she looks stunning—which she will—in her cotton candy-pink tights, and do it with a smile and not even a hint of an eye-roll. And when attempting to muster up ever more enthusiasm for *that* color, it may help to remember that in 14 years when she's going through her all-black goth stage, you'll pine for these rosy days.

Book it!

Watch her race upstairs for bedtime stories when you promise her a reading of *Pinkalicious*, a book about a girl who loves the color so much she turns pink herself.

Show Me the Monet!

You can cut a relatively straight line and sort of color in the lines. Picasso, you are not. Your daughter, however, will beg you to spend untold hours snipping, sorting, scribbling, painting, and pasting with her. And don't even get us started on glue and glitter. She'll amass more art supplies in her little life than you imagine every kid in your grade school owned collectively. Why? Because art is a form of self-expression, one little girls often love intuitively the way they love ponies and feather boas. You don't have to know how to use all of these tools right off the bat; half of the fun is exploring this wondrous creative world together—and your daughter will likely take the lead. You might even find yourself delightfully inspired when you're faced with a blindingly white sheet of butcher paper and a rainbow of scented markers.

To help you foster her inner artist, here are some crafty tips to help you think outside the (Crayola) box:

- Glue sticks are a fabulous, mess-less invention— but they dry out in about 35 seconds. Buy 'em in bulk and do your best to keep tabs on the tops.

- Get her a smock—and use it religiously. Even "washable" markers have been known to leave ghastly stains on formerly pristine dresses. You can spring for a fancy floral apron or a rubber painting smock—but an old t-shirt (yours or hers) works just fine, too.

Note: If it's covered with paint or glue when you're done, *do not pull it over her head*. Instead, cut it up the back, roll it up, and throw it away. Contrary to what you might think, your wife will thank you for this.

- Glitter lingers for weeks and glue has a nasty habit of spreading itself *everywhere*. To wit: outside is a great place to do art projects.

- You'll go through approximately 6 miles of tape a week, so buy the cheap, generic kind—and save the pricey, velvet-finish Scotch tape for wrapping presents.

- For a fun and no-clean-up art project on sunny days, all you need are some paint brushes and a cup of water. Take her out to the patio, sidewalk, or driveway and take turns "painting" pictures before your masterpieces disappear in the sun. Pure magic!

- Sidewalk chalk is great for an impromptu game of hopscotch or a few rounds of tic-tac-toe. Another option: Have her lie snow-angel style on the ground and trace her body.

Then take turns designing "outfits" for her body double. Rumor has it that Coco Chanel started this way.*

• Girls love stickers of any kind, and there's no need to buy the fancy ones. Buy holiday stickers (Easter, Halloween, Valentine's Day, Christmas) the day after, or stock up on those cheap, multicolored dots that come in huge packs at office supply stores. Best of all, you'll finally have a use for those free address labels you're always getting in mail—she won't care that your name is misspelled!

• If you're short on supplies, your local super-store or art-supply store will have rubber-handled scissors, fun hole punches, a roll of butcher-style white paper, disposable paint strips, and even fun extras like feathers or googly eyes. Voilà! Rainy day fun is all taken care of.

• Self-adhesive postage stamps look just like stickers to her. Explain the difference early on (or lock up the former in your desk), lest you find your daughter proudly presenting you with the $47 poster she just made.

* Okay, fine, this is made up. But doesn't it sound cool?

Fun coloring fact!

You probably felt like you won the lotto back when your mom bought you your first mega-box of crayons—the one with 64 colors and a built-in sharpener and everything! Did you know that Crayola just keeps churning out new colors like nobody's business? In fact, when Crayola launched in 1908—which we realize was *way* before your time—the first box contained a measly eight shades. By 1971, they were up to 64. Today the range features a mind-numbing 120 hues with names ranging from Asparagus to Wisteria. (Good luck telling the difference between Fuzzy Wuzzy Brown and Beaver, too.)

Advanced trivia

The most popular Crayola colors of all time are Blue (introduced in 1909), Cerulean (a turquoise shade launched in 1990), and Purple Heart (1997).

Pop quiz

Can you spot the fake? All of these are actual Crayola colors . . . except one. Can you guess which one it is?

- Apricot
- Outer Space
- Mulberry
- Sepia
- Razzle Dazzle Rose
- Macaroni and Cheese

- Artichoke Heart

- Manatee

- Inchworm

*Answer: Artichoke Heart is NOT a Crayola color, even though
it should be.*

Clothes Make the Girl

Random guy: "Honey, what am I going to wear tonight?"

Female partner: "Khakis, blue button-down, white undershirt, brown shoes."

Random Guy: "Belt or no belt?"

Female partner: (Heavy sigh.) "Belt. With the shirt *tucked in*."

Okay, you very well may be capable of dressing yourself—that was just an exaggerated example of the fashion-phobia that many guys actually do suffer (or the overbearing fashion sense their female companions may posses). If it seems like your wife was born just *knowing* this stuff, there's a reason: she was.

Likewise, your budding fashionista is likely to have very particular ideas about what does and doesn't look good when it comes to her closet. When she sneaks into her room and changes her outfit for the 37th time of the day, remember that what she puts on her body is yet another way she has of expressing and exercising her creative freedom, testing limits, and earning approval. As such, trust us when we tell you that trying to convince her that the orange skirt looks better without the purple tights won't score you any points. (If you're scratching your head right now and wondering, *"What difference does it make?"* you've got a definite head start here.)

Some tips on attire

- When dressing your daughter is on your to-do list, DO occasionally offer her some acceptable options. "Do you want the red dress or the pink skirt today?" can shave a half hour off of the dressing process and possibly stave off a meltdown.

- DON'T give her a choice every time—this gives her the false impression that she will always have a say in her wardrobe, which she won't.

- DO choose your clothing battles. Say you're taking her for a walk on a beautiful, sunny day, and she wants to wear her rain boots. Who cares? Save the insistence for the day she wants to don flip-flops and a tutu during a hailstorm.

- DON'T forget about seasonal-appropriateness. Many a mom has been known to lament to her friends about "the time Daddy sent Sally to preschool in her parka . . . in July." (See the bit about pre-selected options, above.)

- DO encourage her to dress herself—and compliment her heartily when she does. Never mind that even *you* know that stripes and polka dots are a fashion match made in hell or that she's chosen to wear her shirt backward. If it's doing the job of covering her body, tell her "well done"—she wants nothing more than your praise. (Score hubby as well as daddy points by installing a child-sized coat rack, pegs, mirror, or whatever other hardware will help her do it herself.)

- DON'T forget about accessories! She may not think she's "dressed" without piles of necklaces, glittery stick-on earrings, and an armful of bangles. Look on the bright side: when she's thusly decked, she'll be easy to spot (and hear) in a crowd.

- DO ask her to help you pick out *your* clothes (this is best done on weekends and work-at-home days). You can tell her she's got great style until you're blue in the face, but this little move proves that you really mean it. Same goes for letting her help pick out a baby sibling's ensemble. ("Which onesie do *you* think looks best?")

• DON'T overlook the value of a dress-up trunk. Having a stash of fun and frivolous frocks on hand that she can put on and take off at will gives you an option when she's itching for a costume change. ("You can put on anything in the dress-up trunk until dinner.")

What's Brewing?

In your world, "tee time" smacks of that bliss-ful moment that kicks off four or more hours on the links. In your daughter's world it's *"tea* time," a phrase that conjures images of miniature cups, raised pinkies, fancy finger foods, and at least a few scalloped doilies (those lacy-looking paper mats you probably remember from Grandma's house). Yes, you will have to engage in this ritual at least a handful of times—but probably many, many more.

Make-believe is one of the most important aspects of a child's development—girl or boy. Whereas a son might choose to fashion every pretzel stick into an Uzi, your daughter is likely to enjoy pretending to be a sophisticated Earl Grey–sipping adult. Research has found that engaging in pretend play can have a positive impact on her language, cognitive, and even social development. (Just don't blame us when your three-year-old demands you take her out for a triple raspberry mocha chai latte.)

T-tip

It's worth noting that tea parties don't necessarily have to involve actual *tea*. (Think about it: hot, bitter beverages aren't usually kiddy crowd-pleasers.) Water, lemonade, apple juice, or even a cup of delicious pseudo-tea (aka air) all work just fine.

Even though few adults you know (younger than 87) still engage in fancy, ritualistic tea parties, the make-believe version is still a staple among the preschool crowd. This is actually a good thing: tea time isn't just a chance for her to play grown-up; it's a chance for you to teach and encourage good table manners.

Turn the tables!

Get creative with the details of your tea parties. Change the location, snacks, theme, or even the guest list. This week can be a formal teddy bear tea; next week you might have a casual, come-as-you-are affair. Pinkies up, Pop!

Now That's Empress-ive!

It's the bane of many parents' existence (in particular the dad half), this fascination with princesses and all their paraphernalia. I mean, *honestly*. Constantly tripping over tiaras and taffeta gowns and glittery, ankle-breaking plastic shoes can get to be a royal pain. Who knew you'd have to teach a preschooler the rule of "No stilettos on the stairs"? And really, what kind of lessons are the princess stories teaching? Wait around (frequently in a coma) for some schmuck to kiss you? Marriage is the ultimate goal? Alas, your P.I.T. (Princess in Training) is bound to be smitten by every fairy tale and fable that crosses her googly-eyed path. The reason (besides the enviable wardrobes): that inescapable happily-ever-after bit. The guaranteed good outcome is incredibly comforting to her. Need convincing? Notice as you're reading one of these stories—even one you've read to her three zillion times before—how downright anxious she'll look at the moment of danger or climax. She *needs* the happy ending, even if it's not the one you'd choose. Try not to think about the fact that most of the princesses go from rags-to-riches courtesy of marrying up. Focus on the positive outcome and the glow of relief on your daughter's perfect face when you reach that last, blissful page.

Here's how to embrace the princess phenomenon without going postal:

- Buy or rent the movie *Mulan*, the animated Disney flick that tells the story of a Chinese maiden who poses as a man to save her family. Not only is the message better than most, but also Mulan's tiny dragon-friend is played by Eddie Murphy, so there are plenty of adult laughs as well.

- Surprise her with a copy of *Do Princesses Wear Hiking Boots?*, a delightful children's book that busts the myth that princesses are prissy.

- Act out favorite fairy-tale scenes with your daughter, rather than succumbing to the whole book or movie. Besides giving you both more active play, it will allow you to mix things up: take turns coming up with new twists to the familiar fables, from making Cinderella into a race-car driver to giving Sleeping Beauty a ridiculously funny snore.

- Suck it up and take her to The Most Magical Place on Earth (you know the one), even arranging for the "lunch with the princesses." Sure, it's expensive, commercialized, and totally over-the-top, but she'll remember the visit forever, with *you* in the role of Prince Charming.

- For some strange and inexplicable reason, the poor princesses' mothers are usually dead in most fairy tales. Feel free to skim gently over this part as you read her stories, or fast-forward to Scene 2 on your DVD. There will be lots of time later to explain fun concepts like divorce, death, and blended families. If your daughter is particularly sensitive to scary scenes, most DVDs—from classic *Cinderella* to contemporary *The Little Mermaid III*—allow you to just listen to the songs, usually the best part. Make it a royal dance party!

- Call her "princess" from time to time, even if it makes you cringe. It's all about her now, Dad, so get used to it.

Use the following cheat sheet to familiarize yourself with her favorite fairy-tale heroines.

The tale	The princess	The problem	The payoff
Cinderella	Cinderella	Wicked stepmother and stepsisters make life awful—until fairy godmother shows up.	Loses glass slipper at ball, prince finds it, and they live happily ever after.
Snow White and the Seven Dwarfs	Snow White	Evil queen is jealous of her beauty and orders her killed; Snow White hides with seven dwarfs in woods.	Queen gives her a poisoned apple that puts her into an eternal coma. Prince finds, kisses, and awakens her . . . and they live happily ever after.
Beauty and the Beast	Belle	Bookish "Beauty" offers her own life for her father's freedom; forced to live in castle with Beast.	Falls in love with Beast—who is actually a prince under an evil spell. Shockingly, they live happily ever after.

The tale	The princess	The problem	The payoff
Aladdin	Jasmine	Princess sneaks out of boring palace to find excitement; falls in love with poor but kind-hearted Aladdin.	Jasmine's dad, the sultan, changes the law so that she can marry the dethroned prince; eternal happiness ensues.
Sleeping Beauty	Aurora	Cursed as a baby to prick her finger on a spinning wheel on her 16th birthday and die; "sleeping beauty" (aka Briar Rose) instead falls into a deep sleep.	Kissed and (of course) awakened by Prince Phillip, with whom she goes on to live . . . oh, you know the rest.
The Little Mermaid	Ariel	Bored, precocious mermaid pines for life on land and makes a deal to exchange her beautiful voice for legs.	Falls in love with Prince Eric, and forsakes the sea to remain human— and a princess. See ending(s), above.

Telling tales

Girls are fascinated with all manner of fables and fairy tales, even when they are a bit out of reach. Alas, some of the classics are Grimm indeed. Spare her the goriest stories—at least for now—and instead make up your own lively tales. Feel free to borrow from the beloved originals—casting, for instance, a girl named Rapunzel with long hair she can send down from a tower in the main role, or creating new adventures for a lass named Thumbelina who sleeps inside a flower petal and rides on the back of a bird. Throw in a little magic from the likes of *Alice in Wonderland* (a heroine who can walk right through a mirror!) and *Wizard of Oz* (ruby slippers and yellow brick roads!) and you'll have her convinced you're the best story-teller of them all.

Valley of the Dolls

With very little exception, girls love their dolls. Watch a toddler toting around her "baby," and you may feel like you're watching a documentary on instinct in the making. She'll name them (often her own name, bless her heart), dress them, push them around in tiny strollers, and pretend to feed, change, and sometimes even nurse them. She gets a kick out of this because all of a sudden, *she's* bigger and more able than someone else—

even if that someone else has "Made in China" etched into her hard, plastic backside.

Oh, baby!

One cool thing about your daughter's interest in baby dolls is that by the time it develops, you'll already be an expert in baby gear (thanks to *her*)! She'll be totally impressed when she watches you skillfully change, dress, and soothe her "baby."

As a guy, you might think that if a child has one or two dolls, that ought to be plenty. The strange thing is, little girls can own dozens of pretend little people and still clamor for more, more, more. Even if they all look identical to you—with their glassy eyes and pursed, bottle-ready lips—she'll be able to distinguish them all, and will rotate them in and out of favor on a whim.

Fun fact

Barbie's *official* name is Barbara Millicent Roberts, and she was born in 1959, making her two years older than her long-time boyfriend Ken. In 2004, Mattel issued a press release announcing that the perfect plastic pair had split up; by 2006 they had reconciled. (We feel your relief.)

Just when you think baby-mania is going to drive you mad, she'll discover Barbie, the picture-perfect pinup gal. You can't fight it, Dad, so don't even try. Even if you ban Babs from the premises, your doll-lover will get her hands on one sooner or later. Can't fathom her fascination? Think about it: Barbie is glamorous! She's got accessories! You can call her a bimbo all you want, but Barbie is *smart*. On any given day, she's a surgeon, sign-language instructor, astronaut, army officer, fashion designer, jet pilot, and the sixth Spice Girl. Plus, she's got a camper, a convertible, a condo, *and* a winter house. The gal knows how to have fun!

When your daughter discovers Barbie, the way she plays with her dolls begins to change. She'll have no interest in taking care of Barbie the way she nurtured her baby dolls; she wants to *be* her. She will imagine herself in countless Barbie situations, and make up hilarious dialogue to go with it. Your job? To be Ken (or Skipper or whoever else your daughter christens you for the day). Focus on Barbie's positives, Dad, and not the worrisome facts of her perpetually perky . . . *feet* or her impossibly small waist. When you engage in this game with her, you help her explore adultlike situations from a safe, playful distance. Like everything else, this too shall pass.

Horns o' Plenty!

Long before she discovers Harry Potter, your little girl may develop a budding interest in mythology— in particular, the fabled unicorn. Plain old standard issue horses are practically magnetic to little girls, with their flowing manes and brushable tails. Add a mysterious element of magical power and a striking spiral horn, and it's easy to see why she'll find unicorns so fascinating. Plus, like mermaids and fairies, it's a creature difficult to pin down in real life—the elusiveness only adding to the appeal.

A brief history

The popular horse-hybrid is a mythological crea-ture that gets its name from the Latin words *unus* ("one") and *cornu* ("horn"). Often depicted as your average pointy-headed steed, the tra-ditional unicorn also sports a billy-goat beard, a lion's tail, and cloven hooves. The idea and image of a horned charger have been around for centuries—and most cultures, from ancient Greece and Rome to Western civilization—recognize one version or other, most of which symbolize grace and goodness.

Impress your daughter by pointing out these uni-corn fast facts:

- One legend suggests that when herding ani-mals for the ark, Noah neglected to round up any unicorns—which is why they do not exist today.

- The horn itself is known as an "alicorn," and was often believed to protect against poison.

- Group several of them together and the collective term is a "blessing of unicorns."

- The Scottish Coat of Arms bears the image of two crowned unicorns.

- Germany's Einhornhöhle (Unicorn Cave) contains the fossilized remains of what is believed to be a unicorn. (Bonus points if you take her there to check it out yourselves.)

Fairy Well, Indeed

Whereas little boys may be drawn to large, fire-breathing monsters, their skirted sisters are apt to prefer tiny, flying pixies. Why? Fairies are like dragons in drag. They're mystical and magical *and* they can fly . . . but they are more feminine and have much better outfits. Instead of setting things aflame and instilling fear, they dart about in an enchanting cloud of magical dust, saving the day (and looking darned adorable in the process). And for a young girl in a big world, there's something very appealing about a small, cute, innocent-looking female entity (not unlike herself) who can wield such power.

There's really no question that she'll want a pair of gossamer wings and a wand of her very own, and you will soon be "turned into" every imaginable creature, plus a few she invents on the spot. Oh, and you may as well buy that limited edition *Tinkerbell* DVD right now. It's a wise investment, as (if you let her) she'll watch it hundreds if not thousands of times.

Fun fairy facts only the coolest dads would know:

- Fairy godmothers save the day in both *Cinderella* and *Sleeping Beauty* (which was convenient, seeing as Cinderella didn't have a mother and Sleeping Beauty was locked away in a castle, far away from hers).

- When she asks where fairies come from, quote J. M. Barrie, author of *Peter Pan in Kensington Gardens*: "When the first baby laughed for the first time, its laugh broke into a thousand pieces, and they all went skipping about, and that was the beginning of fairies." (Aw, come on. It's *sweet*.)

- Fairies have always been a popular subject for artists, particularly during the Victorian era.

- Although she played only a small supporting role in the original *Peter Pan*, Tinkerbell is considered the unofficial mascot of the Walt Disney empire. Rest assured your little fairy will recognize both Tink and the Disney logo shortly after she learns to speak.

- According to Disney's website, spunky little Tink's favorite snack is a nice pumpkin muffin. Who knew?

Tutu Much?

Ballerinas are graceful and gorgeous. They twirl and leap and wear fluttery little tutus and lots and lots of pink. They've got neat shoes. Of *course* she's enamored. You, maybe not so much. Chances are you're not going out of your way to watch classical dance. If your wife were bold enough to suggest attending a performance where guys prance about in tights (which she probably wouldn't), you might even consider scheduling some sort of elective surgery for the same evening, just so you could get out of it. (In that case, it may help to know that ballet first emerged in the 15th century Renaissance court of Italy as a dance interpretation of fencing. Perhaps if you imagine the stocking-clad dancers brandishing swords as they arabesque it would seem less . . . girly). Now that you've got a daughter, you can count on at least one—but possibly dozens—of *Nutcracker* performances in your future. Might as well try to psych yourself up for it.

When your dancing queen begs for lessons, sign her up—and then go to the studio and watch her perfect her pirouette. Ballet will help her flexibility, strength, balance, coordination, and posture. Plus, the recitals are sure to melt your heart on the spot.

Some basic ballet terms to share (and practice!) with your daughter:

- **ARABESQUE** (*aa-rah-BESK*): a position involving standing on one leg with the other extended back, knee straight

- **BARRE** (*bar*): a fancy French name for the, well, *bar* where ballerinas warm up

- **DEMI** (*dem-EE*): half or small; usually added to a position name (e.g., demi-arabesque) to indicate a lesser version

- **DERRIÈRE** (*der-ee-AIR*): to the rear (and also making sure you were still paying attention)

- **ELEVÉ** (*ay-leh-VAY*): to rise

- **JETÉ** (*jeh-TAY*): to leap from one foot to the other

- **PLIÉ** (*plee-AY*): a smooth and continuous knee bend

Buy the book

Tiny dancers go bananas for the *Angelina Ballerina* book series, featuring a (sometimes) graceful little mouse who pines to be a prima. Good, clean fun—even if Angelina *does* occasionally sneak out of the house. (Bad mouse.)

- **RELEVÉ** (*reh-leh-VAY*): rising from any position to balance on one or both feet; literally means "lifted"

- **TENDU** (*TOHN-dew*): literally, "to stretch"

Ariel View

By this point, you may have drawn a very simple conclusion: your daughter likes pretty things. Ever seen a homely mermaid? Enough said. Beyond their invariably lush locks, sea sirens inhabit a fascinating underwater world filled with sunken treasures and the luxury of weightless travel. They are naturally curious and are easily enthralled by otherwise mundane earthly para-phernalia like forks and watches. They're graceful and gorgeous and can communicate with spunky dolphins, treacherous whales, and cantankerous little crabs. They sing beautifully and defy their parents. What's not to love?

Her tails-down favorite of all merfolk will be Ariel, also known as the Little Mermaid. Although *The Little Mermaid* was the creation of poet Hans Christian Anderson back in 1836, the original version is a bit scary for little ones, even if it is beautifully written. Disney, of course, retold the story in movie form in 1989, giving it that happily-ever-after ending your daughter adores. She'll want to be the Disney version of Ariel for Halloween at least once—and she'll *insist* on having the orangey-red synthetic wig to boot. Hop on the mer-train by renting the movie (heck, might as well buy it) and learning a few of the songs. She'll swoon when you croon along as handsome Prince Eric to her enchanting Ariel. Then, make a game of seeing who can spot the most cinematic slip-ups. The website IMDB (Internet Movie Database) lists dozens; here's a taste:

- After Ariel and Flounder escape from the shark, Ariel is carrying a bag over her shoulder;

when Ursula is watching from her cave, the bag is gone.

- As she's sleeping in Prince Eric's castle, alternate shots of Ariel show her both on top of and beneath the covers.

- In one dining scene, Ariel's fork sometimes has three prongs; other times it has four.

- In the "Kiss the Girl" scene, Ariel's hair is pulled half back with a bow, but her reflection in the water shows her wearing a ponytail.

- After Prince Eric's dog licks Ariel's cheek, she dreamily rubs the wrong cheek.

De-tales

- In the Hans Christian Anderson version of the story, the Little Mermaid indeed falls in love with the prince—but he goes on to marry someone else. Her choice then is to kill the prince in order to become a mermaid once again (something she cannot bring herself to do), or throw herself into the ocean and dissolve into sea foam, which is her fate. (Clearly not Disney material.) A statue commemorating her sits in Copenhagen harbor.

- The mermaid myth goes back to ancient Greece and the Middle East, where archaeologists have found bronze mermaid statues that are 3,000 years old.

- Planning a trip to Florida? Take her to Weeki Wachee Springs, a one-of-a-kind underwater theater on the Gulf Coast where tail-sporting beauties perform magical mermaid shows. Check out weekiwachee.com for park information, photos, and more.

- The jury's still out on whether or not mermaids actually exist. But think about it: the world (like the ocean) is a big place—and we're learning new things about it all the time. Remember when we used to think Pluto was a planet? Silly us. Maybe someday we'll be saying, "Remember when we thought mermaids were imaginary?" You never know.

- If you're ever going to spring for a pair of swim fins, pony up and get the single-fin mermaid style. Amazon.com sells several different models, any of which is sure to delight your little siren.

- In case there's a quiz: a half-dude, half-fish is called a merman.

Get crafty, land-lubber

Measure your daughter from waist to feet and cut a mermaid-tail shape out of a piece of felt, an old sheet, or any other fabric you have lying around. Leave a long, narrow belt-like portion horizontally at the top. Have her tie it on like a backwards apron, dragging the tail behind her. Bonus points for helping her decorate it with shimmery sequin "scales"!

Make some mini-fins

Place one of her Barbie dolls on a doubled-up piece of construction paper or felt, trace around her from waist to feet, and add a sweeping tail. Cut out the two pieces, staple or glue them up the sides and around the bottom of the tail, and then slip them over the doll for an instant mermaid metamorphosis. Be prepared for your daughter's head to spin in ecstatic circles.

Do You Believe in Magic?

Repeat after us: "Aba-cadabra! Magica-boula! Bibbity-bobbity-boo!" Start practicing now because there's a 99.8 percent chance (actual figure) that your daughter will develop an interest in—or possibly even full-blown obsession with—all things bewitching. She'll make "magic potions" out of anything you give her (or sand, water, and leaves, if left to her own devices), beg you to save the discarded cardboard paper towel tubes (to fashion into magic wands, of course), and cast all manner of spells (some benevolent, others that may border on foreboding) on friends, family, pets, and the occasional innocent frog. Don't fret about her interest in illusion; pretending to be powerful helps her feel secure in her increasingly expanding world. At one time, you too probably pined for the power to wave your hand and make things appear and disappear. Your job now: to encourage, participate, and even console—like when the stubborn toad refuses to morph into a dashing prince. ("This one must be broken, sweetie! Let's go see if we can find another one . . . ")

Ready to make magic?

Master a few simple tricks and you're good to go:

Thumbs up: Even if your daughter never gets into the magic wand thing, now that you're a dad, you *have* to learn "the thumb trick." Make a fist with your left hand, then extend your pointer finger out straight. Next hook your left thumb over the top of the middle finger on the same hand, then wrap your pointer finger over the top of your thumb. Now tuck your right thumb into your palm and wrap the other fingers on that hand around it, fist-style. Place your two hands together so that it looks like the left thumb is actually the right. When your daughter announces "aba-cadabra," pull your hands apart—creating the illusion that you've pulled the tip of your right thumb off. (Don't forget to put it back together afterward, or your daughter could be traumatized for life.)

Ring it on: Hold up a toothpick for her to inspect, and tell her that when she waves her wand, you're going to make it disappear. As she's waving and chanting her magic words, begin wringing your hands together for effect. As casually as you can, slip the toothpick through your wedding band on the *outside* of your hand, then quickly present your (empty) palms for her inspection. Ask her to repeat the chant, wring your hands some more, and make the toothpick "reappear."

On the money: Place several coins of the same denomination in a bowl or bag, ask her to choose one, and write her initial on it with a Sharpie. Wait for the ink to dry, then have her hold the coin tightly in her hand and concentrate on it for a good minute. Close your eyes and have her drop her coin back into the bag or bowl; shake or mix it up well. Reach in with your eyes still closed and easily find the *warm* coin (the one she was holding)!

In the cards: Take a regular old deck of playing cards, and note which card is on the bottom. Fan out the cards and ask your daughter to pick one out, memorize it, and place it on top of the deck. Cut the deck (placing the bottom half on top of "her" card) and then make a great production of neatening up the pile. Then flip the deck over and fan it out—her card will be the one right before the one that was on the bottom to begin with. Presto, Pop!

Commando craft tip

No magic wand handy? Make your own. Draw a star on a piece of sturdy cardboard, cut it out, and wrap it neatly with tin foil. Glue or tape it to the end of a stick or discarded paper towel roll, and cover *that* part with foil as well. Add glitter, feathers, streaming ribbons, or any other pretty "notions" (a girly term for adornments) you can find. So simple, it's almost spooky.

Sparkle...
Plenty!

When it comes to, well, pretty much everything in your little love's life, there's one simple rule you must memorize: if it's not pink, it darned well better sparkle. Seriously. Yes, you'll probably be able to coerce her into wearing brown cords or camo fatigues—just as long as there are some rhinestone studs on them somewhere. Likewise, that navy blue sweatshirt may need to be spruced up with a glittery heart design (craft stores sell handy iron-on patches—and we *know* you can manage an iron), and those plain white sneakers will surely require reflective silver laces. In her little world, sparkles seduce, glitter beckons, and there's just no such thing as razzle-dazzle overdose. All this shimmer makes her feel impossibly fancy, and fancy gets *noticed*. People comment when she's elaborately bejeweled. Attention is good. Enjoy her desire to be in the spotlight now—because someday she may be hiding under chin-length bangs and begging to be left alone. (Probably not, but you never know.)

Ready to shine? Here's a crash course in flair for admittedly dull dudes:

Be brilliant: Hop onto eBay and score a killer deal on a BeDazzler, the original "stud and rhinestone setter." (We're going old-school on you here; your sister probably had one when you were kids.) Buck up, tough guy—there's nothing wussy about crafting when your kid's involved, and the BeDazzler is an actual tool. This nifty little gizmo is as fun and easy to operate as a staple gun (for real), and offers a quick-and-dirty way to add a dash of glitz to an otherwise boring scrap of fabric (think hat, jeans, beach bag . . . the options are endless). She'll shine brighter than a 10-karat cubic zirconia when she sees you wielding this machine in her honor—and the look of shock and awe on your wife's face when you unveil your masterpieces will be worth ten times the BeDazzler's $12 (gently used) price tag.

Extra, extra: read all about it! If you haven't discovered *Fancy Nancy* books yet, set yourself up with a stack. The series' heroine is a precocious little pixie who tirelessly tries to teach her ultra-dull family how to be posh. ("That's a fancy word for fancy.") Your glamour girl will especially love *Fancy Nancy's Famous Fancy Words: From Accessories to Zany* for making learning so lavishly fun.

Circle time: Here's an easy, glittery project she'll love—and you'll ace, because you already know how to do it! What you'll need: clear plastic cups, glue, glitter, and paper plates. To do it: squirt some liquid glue (like Elmer's) onto a paper plate, then dump some glitter onto another one. Dip the rim of one of the plastic cups into the glue and then into the glitter. (You know, as if you were salting a margarita glass. See how handy that skill comes in?) Repeat with as many cups as you have. After letting them dry, let her customize the cups with permanent markers, stickers, or ribbon. She'll love using them to store her beads, pebbles, pennies, hair ties, accessories, lip-gloss, and all of the many other tiny items she's apt to squirrel away. (More on that later.) And while she may think her glitter-rimmed designs would make festive tea cups, it's *your* job to make sure she understands that they are for decorative purposes only.

Skirting the Issue

Imagine this scenario: it's your turn to chauffeur her highness to one of her preschool pal's birthday parties. (If said friend is another little girl, we're going to go out on a limb here and guess the theme will be "princess.") You absentmindedly pull a pair of jeans from her dresser—and watch in horror as she begins to melt down before your very eyes. Between the sniffling and the gasping, you think you hear her mutter something that sounds like *"flocked lamé,"* but since those can't possibly be actual words, you're totally in the dark.

You know how your wife can change her clothes 13 times when trying to decide what to wear for a night out? Well, here's a newsflash, Pop: the apple doesn't fall far from the tree. Saying that females (of any age) can be particular about their party attire is like saying tax return forms can be tedious.

In your daughter's little mind, a party means three things: a guaranteed cupcake, a possible parting gift, and an excuse to put on the fanciest frock she owns. Grasping this in advance—and not trying to convince her she'll "have more fun" or "be more comfortable" in her regular old play clothes—shows her that you truly understand her, in all of her eccentric, bewildering glory.

What are the essential features of a party dress? Well, it's usually long, often with a full skirt, and almost always has a big, fancy bow in the back. It can be any color (pink) or material—as long as it makes a delightful swishy sound when she walks. In a perfect world, it's conveniently machine-washable (this information will be on the tag) because while she'll love the idea of proper attire, she surely has no intention of *acting* proper when she's in it.

Your task: help her choose from among the several gowns undoubtedly hanging in her closet, and tell her the one she picks is simply perfect. Let her wear the tiara and boa with it, if she wants (it's not *your* fault if she upstages the birthday girl—it's not like it's a wedding or anything). And the sparkly *Wizard of Oz* shoes (or polka-dot rain boots), even if they don't match. Fawn appropriately, and when party time comes, be sure to say, "Your chariot awaits!"

Cache Value

Not to get too science-y on you, but evolutionary psychologists pretty much agree that in the old hunter–gatherer societies, it was typically the men doing the hunting and the women doing the gathering. As soon as your daughter masters the infamous "pincer grasp," these natural instincts are well on their way to kicking in. Soon enough, you'll be tripping over collections of everything under the sun, stashed in bags, bottles, bowls, cups, and anything else that can function as a carryall. Rocks, seashells, stickers, leaves, marbles, paper clips, coins, buttons, beads, scraps of paper, pack-ing peanuts, even petrified crumbs can be excit-ing if she's able to gather a decent pile of them.

Sometimes it will be enough simply to hoard great quantities of similar objects. Other times, the assembled bits and pieces will have a greater purpose—usually in the form of an elaborate art project (likely a 3-D nature diorama you'll have to figure out where to display and how to dispose of later).

Building a collection sharpens several skills, including selecting, identifying, evaluating, clas-sifying, and arranging. If she's got the organiz-ing gene, the drive to stockpile may turn into a lifelong love of collecting. She may one day own a rare and priceless stamp or coin collection—and she'll have *you* to thank for your eager support.

Embrace her inner pack rat with these fun activities:

- Fill a big metal bowl with an assortment of dried beans (lentils, black beans, kidney beans, etc.). Then get an empty egg carton, ice cube tray, or cupcake pan and help her sort them into like kinds. Marvel at her painstaking patience and dexterity.

- Try the same game above with a big bag of buttons (craft stores sell them by the hundreds in random assortments). See how many different ways she can sort them: by color, size, shape, number of thread holes, ones she likes/dislikes, etc.

- Get her a little magnetic board and start collecting silly souvenir magnets from places you visit. Since magnets are inexpensive, this is a great way to affordably memorialize your travels. Gradually add in magnetic paper dolls, letters, and numbers.

- Come up with something unique to collect together, such as heart-shaped rocks, green sea glass, or pennies that were coined the year she was born. (Note: Choose something that's not so common as to be considered "unworthy" or that will be too cumbersome to store, yet not so obscure as to make the search frustrating.)

- Take her to a museum or library and discuss the "collections." Ask her how she thinks the items are grouped and sorted, and inquire about her favorites. Watch her grow two full inches when you ask her opinion.

Money-saving tip for savvy stockpilers

Never throw away plastic jars with lids, small candy tins, or shopping bags (including gently used Ziploc bags). Saving and stashing these castoffs where she can get to them can save you thousands of dollars in container costs over her lifetime.

Under Statements

For most guys, the undergarment issue boils down to a single, simple decision: boxers or briefs. Your darling daughter, however, is apt to be far less blasé about her unmentionables. And why shouldn't she be? To her, skivvies represent freedom (from diapers!), independence (she can put them on and take them off *herself*, thank-you-very-much), and good old-fashioned comfort (can you imagine trotting around in a swollen, saggy nappy all day?). Like her outerwear, they also serve as a chance to express herself. You're darn tootin' she wants them to be cute.

As a necessary accessory, underpants can be a potential area of conflict—if you don't grasp a few simple rules. These do's and don'ts should help:

- DON'T try to convince her that what's on the front doesn't matter. *It does*. This doesn't mean she'll never want to wear the snowman panties in July, it just means she'll have an opinion about it. Get used to it.

- DO keep (several) backup pairs in your car and travel bag for outings. You might even consider stashing some new, never-seen-before models there. Accidents happen, and when they do she's likely to be upset. A generous selection of replacement options can diffuse a meltdown beautifully.

- DON'T worry if she insists on wearing her "days of the week" panties on the wrong days. Her preschool teachers have seen *everything*, and they won't think you're a bad dad, we promise.

- DO let her wear the ruffled panties, even though you think they look impossibly uncomfortable. It probably won't be the last time she sacrifices comfort for fashion.

- DON'T forget to make sure she's wearing panties before leaving the house, even if you put them on her yourself just minutes before. Undies have a strange habit of disappearing into thin air. Trust us on this one.

In brief

The first time you find yourself charged with the task of purchasing new panties could also inspire your first panic attack. Thwart it by mastering this simple breakdown of style options before you head out:

- **BIKINI:** itsy bitsy, teeny weeny underpants

- **BLOOMERS:** big, pouffy "granny panties" (bloomers often come with a matching dress)

- **BRIEFS:** standard tighty-whities for girls (don't let the "whitie" part fool you; briefs can be any color of the rainbow—or all of them)

- **BOY SHORTS:** just as the name implies; picture longer, larger briefs

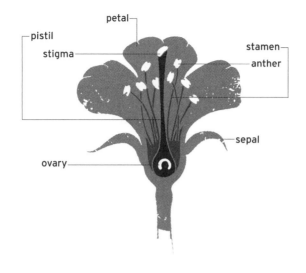

Flower Power!

You know how elated your wife is when you surprise her with a bouquet of flowers? (If the answer to that question is "Not really," or "Never done it," put down this book and get yourself to a florist. The woman is the mother of your child, for heaven's sake. She deserves some foliage.) Well, your daughter is likely to be just as smitten with anything in the flora family. Why? Flowers are like nature's candy: they look *and* smell irresistible. She'll love to clip beautiful blossoms, collect them, arrange them, press them, even taste them (so be sure to point out precisely what is and isn't edible if you've got any greenery around).

You can encourage your budding botanist's innate enthusiasm by planting something together. Even if you don't have room for a full-scale garden, certainly you can find a spot for a potted plant or two. This is your chance to introduce her to the delights of dirt, Dad—and you don't need a green thumb to do it.

Get up and grow!

Sunflowers are a great first plant because they are inexpensive, shoot up quickly, and the resulting bloom packs plenty of wow-power. Plus, the seeds are big and easy to handle, so she can do the planting all by her little self. If you've got the space outside, look for the words "mammoth," "giant," or "tall" when shopping for sunflower seeds; those suckers get *huge*. If you're planting indoors, look for the smaller "Elf" or "Teddy" varieties. Plant them where they'll get lots of sun (and after the last frost, if you're going alfresco) and keep the soil moist but not soggy. When the sunflower blooms, you can actually toast and eat the seeds—if neighborhood birds haven't gotten to them yet. To do it, snip the head about two inches down the stem and hang it upside down until it is completely dry. Loosen the seeds by gently rubbing, and then soak them overnight in salted water. In the morning, drain the water, spread them on a baking sheet, and roast for three hours at 200°F. (You can also save some seeds before you roast to plant again.) Nature teacher, activity creator, and snack provider—see how industrious you are?

Take a hike

Pack a small pair of (child-friendly) scissors and a handled shopping bag and hit a local trail. Within reason, encourage her to snip the stalks of anything she thinks is lovely and put it into the bag. (If you're not already familiar with poison oak and ivy, you might want to Google those before you head out.) This can also be done in the backyard.

When you get home, help her arrange her clippings into a charming centerpiece for Mom.

Know your parts

Save one of the blooms you find on your hike and help her diagram it, identifying all of the parts; she'll think you're super-smart and dig (pun intended) the time together.

The flower part	What it does
petal	attracts insects and other pollinators
anther	makes pollen
stamen	provides support
sepal	protects developing flower bud
stigma	traps pollen
pistil	gets pollen to ovary
ovary	holds egg cells

Kiss and Makeup

You probably look at your daughter's fresh, innocent face and see stunning perfection. Those rosy cheeks, full pink lips, and impossibly long lashes are clearly the stuff of poetry. Naturally the first time she spackles her eyelids with iridescent blue powder and smears the entire vicinity around her mouth with glittery, scarlet goop, you might be shocked and appalled. Remember, Dad: she thinks she looks beautiful, and you'd better believe that barking "What on *earth* is all over your face?" is not quite the reaction she's hoping for.

You certainly don't have to like her dabbling in premature face-painting, and obviously, you are not going to let her out of the house in all of her made-up glory for many, many (*many*) years. If her mom is the fresh-faced type, you may not even have to engage in the lip-gloss battles for a decade or more. But if your miniature runway model is fascinated with cosmetics and comes by her inclination honestly, the last thing you want to do is forbid them outright—unless your unwitting goal is to make makeup even more alluring.

Seeing as it is Mom's makeup stash she's likely to be pilfering from, odds are that your wife may have already established some cosmetic ground rules. (Think, "Eyeliner is for *eyes*, not walls," "We wipe lipstick off our hands with paper towels, not Mommy's bathrobe," "Leave this house looking like a clown and you're grounded for a year.") Your job is to go with the flow, compliment her natural beauty ("You don't need that stuff to be beautiful, honey!" or "I think you look perfect just the way you are!"), and put up with her cosmetic experimentations that fall within your preset guidelines. Here's how to suck it up when the blush brush comes out:

- Use your manly skills to build (or assemble) a vanity table for her. The prefabricated kind frequently come with "pretend" makeup, which she'll spend hours "applying" without any visible damage.

- Wielding a simple lip balm (think Chapstick or Burt's Bees) can make her feel grown-up and glamorous. Many feature all-natural ingredients and no tint whatsoever, so what's the harm? It can even help soothe her dry lips in the winter. Find one with a tube you think she'll like, call it lipstick, and tell her she's old enough to keep it on her nightstand—it's a big deal. (Just be sure it's kept out of reach of younger siblings who will invariably try to eat it.)

- A tiny jar of *extremely* subtle shimmered powder will resemble a pot of gold to her. (Drug stores sell them cheap.) Under your strict supervision, allow her to dust her cheeks and nose and marvel at the stunning results.

- Try not to gag (audibly) when she gets her first Makeup Doll Head. These little joys have been around forever—ask your wife about hers—and the benefit, of course, is that it's not her own face (or yours) that's being "beautified." You'll appreciate this at some point.

Your
Burgeoning
Bag Lady

If you think your wife has a lot of purses, wait until you see the collection of carryalls your young daughter will have amassed by her fifth birthday. From flimsy grocery bags (paper or plastic; she's not particular yet) to Granny's gaudy old tissue-carriers to sequin princess pouches, if she can stash something in it—even a penny and a paper clip—she'll simply have to have it.

Let's revisit our ancestral past again: men hunt, women gather. It's just in our natures. So if she's hardwired to collect stuff, naturally she's going to need a vessel to carry it in. It just makes sense, right?

The part that might make less sense to you is the fact that she *can never have too many purses*. You see, there's really no such thing. Try to reason with her ("These two are identical in every way!") and she's likely to turn tactical on you ("Exactly! So it's okay if I lose one!"). There's no winning, so don't even try.

For the next decade or so, you will find these totes strewn about your living space and marvel at the absolutely random contents: this one will have four rocks and a rubber band; that one will hold two jacks, a half-eaten apple, a broken flashlight, and a sock. As you sort through these bizarre collections each night, remember: *she's just doing her job*.

Sack it to her!

Beyond the backpack and the duffel bag, your knowledge of bag styles is likely to be rather limited. Impress her by offering up these terms; they might even come in handy if there's ever a missing-clutch emergency:

- **BUCKET:** a roomy bag resembling a pail, with an open top and single shoulder strap

- **CLUTCH:** a small purse with no handle or strap that is either carried in hand or under the arm

- **FANNY PACK:** a small pouch worn on a belt around the waist (Note: She might look cute in one of these; you *never, ever* will.)

- **HOBO:** a large, soft bag that scrunches down when set down

- **MINAUDIÈRE:** a small, fancy (beaded or sequin, perhaps) evening bag (Note: No one we know actually uses this term, but it sounds so very fancy.)

- **MUFF:** a fur (real or fake) or velvet bag with "pockets" you slip your hands into to warm them

- **SATCHEL:** a bag of any size that has a wide, flat bottom and two straps (picture a doctor's bag)

- **TOTE:** a rectangular bag with a flat bottom, open top and two handles—as in a shopping or beach bag

Bag to the future

Researchers have found that the average 30-year-old woman owns 21 handbags and buys a new one every 3 months. No wonder your wife's always pining for a bigger closet.

The Mane Event

Few aspects of parenting a little girl are more daunting to some dads than the matter of hair (at least until she hits dating age—but no use getting ourselves worked up over that just yet). Even if you yourself are more Fabio than Dennis Franz, the sheer volume of hair accessories gals have to choose from is enough to have you reaching for the Flowbee. (Yup, they still make those combo vacuum-hair clippers. And don't get any ideas.)

Whoever decided the crew cut wasn't a good look for girls, anyway?

Your daughter may well go through an extended "I can do it myself" hair phase, for which you (if not her mother) will be eternally grateful. During this phase, she may insist on trying to squeeze every available hair accessory she owns onto her head. As adorable as this is, eventually there may come a day when you're entrusted (read possibly forced) to coerce her hair into something resembling a style. Possibly even one your wife deems "acceptable." Think of this section as your new best "don't go near the vanity table without me" friend.

Some tips to minimize tress distress:

- Wash and condition her hair daily, or as close to it as humanly possible. Trying to skip this step on "daddy night" will only result in delayed trouble. The conditioner is key as it helps minimize the tangling that makes brushing or combing pure torture (for both of you). You might also invest in a detangler spray, making the comb-through a lot easier.

- Mom will probably be on top of this, but just in case: be sure your daughter gets regular trims as this will help prevent bothersome snarls too.

- Discover the joys of "leave-in" conditioner, and do please note that unless a conditioner says "leave-in" right on the bottle, you must rinse it out.

- Expect a painstakingly crafted "hairstyle" to last approximately 5 minutes. This is all part of the process, and trying to fight it is as effective as repeatedly banging your head on a nearby wall.

- Just about any hairdo you execute (except when all or some of the hair is pulled straight back into some sort of fastener) will need to have a part. A part, practically by definition, vaguely resembles a straight line that neatly divides the hair and is most easily achieved using a comb rather than a brush. Work on this.

When you're playing stylist, keep this glossary of hair terms handy:

- **PONYTAIL:** all hair brushed back into one rubber band, which, inexplicably, should *never* be made of actual rubber (Note: Those suckers are impossible to get out. Softer, fabric-covered bands are a must.)

- **PIGTAILS:** two ponytails positioned (roughly) opposite each other on either side of her head

- **BUTTERFLY CLIP:** a hinged plastic clip with jaw-like teeth that come together to hold hair in place; a great starter accessory as these are relatively easy to manipulate for both of you

- **HEADBAND:** a hard (half circle) or soft (full circle) band used to pull hair back and away from her face (Note: If using the soft kind, slip the *entire band* completely over her head first, and pull the hair in the back out of it so that the band is underneath her hair at her nape. Otherwise she'll have a John McEnroe thing going and your wife will *not* approve.)

- **BARRETTE:** a hinged hair clasp with two sides that clamp together to hold a portion of hair

- **BOBBY PINS:** similar to barrettes but without a clasp, bobby pins simply slide into hair and stay put because of the tight, spring-load design (Note: These are actually harder to manipulate than barrettes; avoid if possible.)

- **SCRUNCHY:** a rubber band that's been wrapped in an excess of fabric for a bunchy, "scrunchy" look; scrunchies often find their way onto wrists, but should never be confused with a bracelet

- **BRAID:** a rope-like design created by systematically weaving together three strands of hair

- **FRENCH BRAID:** a much more complicated version of the basic braid, created by starting with one small section of hair (divided into three even smaller sections) and adding a "new" section to each one as you braid them (Note: Unless you went to beauty school, chances are this style won't make it into your repertoire.)

- **BUN:** A ponytail that's been twisted and clipped up and around the base, forming a circular knot; it's worth noting that messy buns are "in" so don't be afraid to attempt this style or some variation of it

Disguise the Limit!

Ever stop to ponder why Halloween is such a popular holiday? Even if the candy part were eliminated (which would be tragic for parents who live for a few stolen Kisses), kids would still partake for the costumes alone. In full regalia, a child almost believes she *is* a pirate/fairy/Jedi/cat/knight/gypsy/Power Ranger. She'll try to walk, talk, sing, and act like the character in question. There's no doubt that dress-up is one of the most powerful forms of creative play—so why save it for Halloween?

Start stockpiling things for her costume trunk now and you'll be ahead of the game. Hit the after-Halloween sales and pick up a rocker or a flapper wig, some fairy wings, a feather boa, and a smattering of tutus. Then scour garage sales or thrift stores for costume jewelry, hats, scarves, and other funky accessories. Even your old ties will be fair game, so when your wife deems one "out of style," you can recycle it directly into the trunk. Nifty, no?

Your daughter may be the all-princess-nothing-but-princess type, or she may have more of a mix-it-up style. (The latter is apt to christen herself a "cowgirl ninja bunny" or a "ballerina witch" by combining random costume parts.) She might be drawn to vampire teeth and Freddy Krueger claws, or she may firmly believe that if the ensemble clashes with her bejeweled tiara, it's not even worth considering. This is all part of the exploratory fun, and says next to nothing about what she'll be like as an adult. Plenty of grown-up tomboys admit to having gone through a frilly phase, and just as many girly-girls rode dirt bikes and tortured ants with magnifying glasses back in the day. Don't read into anything, Dad. She's just having fun.

Take her hunting ... for junk!

For a fun-and-cheap daddy/daughter activity, nothing beats the Saturday morning garage sale circuit. (Stop by Starbucks first; you'll need it.) Give her a small amount of cash—say, $2—and have her see how many cool dress-up odds and ends she can score. (Think clip-on earrings for a dime; fabulously gaudy handbags for a buck.) Mom will appreciate the break and you'll earn bonus points for accidentally slipping in a little math lesson. Later on, you'll get great joy from teaching her the art of haggling—and then watching her work it.

Make-believe you can

Once your costume trunk is thusly stuffed—and you're mostly familiar with the contents—make up characters and have her decide what they should wear. Give them funny names (such as "Tutu, Queen of the Rodents") and encourage her to concoct the craziest outfit possible.

Dress-up detail

Ancient dads weary of princess paraphernalia had it a lot easier than you do: early Halloween costumes were mostly of the ghoulish variety (think skeletons, witches, devils, and ghosts). The reason? To scare off evil spirits, of course. (Hence, a nice pair of fairy wings just wouldn't do.)

Tired of the dress-up clean-up?

Play "paper" dolls with her. The best sets feature sturdy *wooden* dolls that come with an easy-to-change magnetic wardrobe. Practice muttering reassuring sentences such as, "Of course I love the high-tops with the wedding gown, dear!"

A Perfect 10 (It's Not What You Think)

The tending to one's finger and toenails may be rituals to which you've never given a passing thought. After all, "nibble, clip, repeat" is pretty hard to improve upon, right?

If you're among the handful of evolved dudes who admit to delighting in the occasional *mani*cure, our apologies for assuming ignorance. But for the majority of the male masses who've never had a stranger scrub their soles or clean up their cuticles, these grooming services may sound more exotic (and less appealing) than a dish of deep-fried grasshoppers.

Like makeup and dress-up and other forms of imaginative play, decking her digits is just another of the many ways your little girl will explore being a *big* girl. It's harmless fun—and a wonderful excuse to get her to sit still for 15 minutes straight.

For the record, no one is suggesting you haul your preschooler to the nearest nail salon for a pricey "mani/pedi" (shorthand for manicure/pedicure), although if you're so inclined, knock yourself out. Otherwise, skip the salon and stay home. You really *can* paint her microscopic fingers and toes yourself for one simple reason: she's pretty darned easy to please. In fact, we can almost promise you that if you can manage to get a swipe of paint anywhere in the area of the nail bed, she'll be tickled.

These polish pointers will get you off on the right foot:

- The lighter the polish shade, the less noticeable it will be when a) it's smeared everywhere, and b) it starts chipping (which will be approximately 30 seconds after you finish painting). A clear formula with a tiny bit of glitter in it looks impressive in the bottle and is extremely forgiving on fingers and toes.

- Always have a paper towel under the hand or foot being painted, and another stack nearby to catch any drips.

- Nail polish is one of the most difficult substances on the planet to clean up once it's spilled (or remove once it's dried on anything other than a human nail). Scheduling nail services in your garage, workshop, or even outside can do wonders for your marriage.

- When it comes to paint on the brush, *less is more*. Pull the wand out of the bottle and swipe it on the inside neck of the bottle several times, rotating the brush as you do this.

Remember, her nails are *tiny*. A small drop is all you need.

- As she's highly likely to forget that her extremities are sporting wet paint, shuffling or keeping her outside after you make manicure magic will minimize damage to your furniture and other belongings.

- Want to really impress her? Pick up a package of nail gems or decals at the drug store. They stick to wet polish like glue and up the fancy-factor at least 300 percent. In fact, sometimes you can skip the polish-part altogether and go straight for the decals. What could be easier than *that*?

Savvy-dad tip

When she's resisting a much-needed nail-clipping, you might try to bribe, er, *persuade* her with the promise of a manicure or pedicure. Hey, sometimes a dad's gotta do what a dad's gotta do.

Face the Music

What do some old guy who plays knick-knack, an extremely small spider who likes to climb water pipes, and a poor woman who croaks after polishing off a pony (among other creatures) have in common? Any day now, you're going to be singing about—or listening to your daughter sing about—all of them. Don't believe it? It's undeniable and unavoidable: if all the world is indeed a stage, your daughter is the star of the show. And did we mention it's a *musical*?

Mastering the art of music is her first taste of the fine arts. She loves familiar songs because—you guessed it—they're *familiar*. Being able to belt out the right words at the right time feels fantastic, and the inevitably delighted response from her audience is all the encouragement she needs to unleash her inner performer.

Now, you *could* expose your daughter to nothing but your own personal iPod playlist. This is a fine idea—until she decides to delight her preschool teachers or the local playgroup with a rousing rendition of (insert your favorite Green Day tune here). Do you think parents everywhere *enjoy* cruising around listening to the Wiggles? Um, not so much. But it's part of the job.

You may think that you are hopelessly clueless when it comes to toddler tunes, but if you dig deep, you might even surprise yourself. Twinkle, twinkle? Old MacDonald? The wheels on the bus?

If you're happy and you know it . . . clap your hands? B-I-N-G-O!

The key to mastering her music is to get into it. She doesn't care if you sing off-key, and messing up the words (or substituting ridiculous ones) is a surefire way to send her into a delicious fit of giggles as she corrects you. When you start to feel self-conscious, remember: you've got the most forgiving audience-slash-backup band on the planet. Rock on, Dad.

Until she's ready to join you for a Wii Rock Band jam sesh, these tips will strike all the right notes:

- Forget trying to memorize all of those pesky lyrics. A perfect dad-daughter game is to take a familiar tune and ad-lib some nonsense words—on the spot. "The squirrels on the fork go crash, bang, boom! Crash, bang, boom!" Ask Mom to decide whose song is the silliest.

- Play "talent show" together. This is less painful than it sounds as she will probably appoint you judge and *herself* the talent.

Make up some score cards (Hint: They should all read "10!"), set up a stage (a coffee table or stair landing works just fine), and cue the diva.

• Dust off the karaoke machine. Few things will delight her more than the sound of her own voice amplified to echoing decibels.

• Learn to tune out. Sounds cruel but trust us: after you've listened to her belt out *Fruit Salad, Yummy Yummy!* 700 times in a row, this is a crucial skill you'll wish you had mastered. (Hint: Smile, nod, and when you hear a break in the action, applaud and whistle appreciatively.)

Animal Magnetism

Even if you and your wife are planning to shower your daughter with siblings, her urge to nurture knows no bounds. Tops on her take-care-of-it list will be small furry babies of any breed or bearing. From aardvarks to zebras, her tiny tender heart will bleed with a need to care for and cuddle it, pet it and protect it. Fortunately for folks who don't live on a farm or in a zoo, there's a plush version of every mammal, fish, amphibian, reptile, and bird on the face of the earth. And she'll want *every last one*.

Don't go getting the crazy notion that you can dissuade her from stockpiling stuffed animals by getting her a living one. Surely she'll love Fluffy or Fido, but she'll still need to stock her imaginary ark with an arsenal of inorganic pets. The love of stuffing is practically a requirement in Little Girl Land. (Ask your wife how many of such friends *she* collected as a kid.) Your daughter will name her wooly babies, host elaborate parties in their honor, pretend to walk and feed them, bandage their imaginary wounds, drag them on countless outings, and sleep with as many as can fit in her bed. And while there is likely to be one top dog among the litter, her preferred pets may also rotate in and out of favor on a whim. (That toy box you were thinking about building? Better upgrade to the bigger model.) The upside: her fuzzy puppy lust makes grabbing a last-minute airport souvenir for her a snap.

Daddy do-right moment

Help her come up with clever names for her brood. Sure, Bunny and Kitty are suitable monikers, but Mitzi Moo Mouse Monkey and Jillian Jellycat Giraffe are *way* better. Nametags, anyone?

From the "Who's coming up with this stuff, anyway?" file

Everyone's heard of a "flock of seagulls" and a "pack of wolves." But did you know that almost every animal group has its very own (often totally random) name? Turn her mammalian fixation into a teaching tool by helping her learn these obscure but accurate terms:

- A **shrewdness** of apes

- A **sleuth** of bears

- A **brace** of bucks

- A **clowder** of cats

- A **quiver** of cobras

- A **kine** of cows

- A **float** of crocodiles

- A **pack** of dogs

- A **pod** of dolphin

- A **pace** of donkeys

- A **gang*** of elk

- A **mob*** of emus

- A **business*** of ferrets

- A **charm** of finches

- A **band** of gorillas

- An **array** of hedgehogs

- A **bloat*** of hippopotami

- A **smack*** of jellyfish

- A **troop** of kangaroos

- A **kindle** of kittens

- A **deceit** of lapwings

- A **watch** of nightingales

- A **family** of otters

- A **parliament*** of owls

- A **pandemonium*** of parrots

- A **run** of poultry

- An **unkindness*** of ravens

- A **crash** of rhinos

- A **dray** of squirrels

- An **ambush*** of tigers

- A **knot** of toads

- A **zeal** of zebras

*Especially funny to say with bonus points for excellent visual imagery

You've Got It Maid!

Alanis Morissette missed this one in her infamous tune, "Ironic": the lovely lady you were lucky enough to marry may lament the nonstop carnival of household chores on her daily to-do list, but your daughter will delight in spending her days pretending to mow, sew, mix, fix, mop, chop, slice, dice, rake, bake, dust, iron, sweep, and fold. (This holds true even if she's never actually seen either of her parents perform any of these tasks. Freaky, huh?) Heck, look at Cinderella! Her tireless toiling (without complaint, even!) landed her smack in the finest castle around. How can household chores not take on a potentially glamorous air?

High-end houseware and toy companies wisely pander to pint-size hausfraus by filling their catalogs with a darling, must-have array of appliances and gadgets in pretty shades of pink and "stainless steel." From rosy refrigerators and bubble-gum blenders to shiny chrome toasters and sleek silver vacuums, these alluring gadgets frequently hum, click, and purr just like the real deal, and they're all delightfully scaled down to *just her size*. Simple or elaborate toy kitchens abound in any toy store, as do all manner of toy foods and cutlery. Playing with all of this stuff is just another way to try on a different grown-up hat—but don't get your hopes up. Her interest in the domestic arts may or may not persist.

When she expresses a burning desire to dust, here's how to encourage these noble pursuits:

- Put her to "work." Even tiny tykes can handle a feather duster, a small handheld vacuum, or a miniature broom and dustpan. She'll love feeling like she's contributing—especially when you pile on the praise for a job well done.

- Whip up something in the kitchen together—Jell-O pudding, sugar cookies, and Rice Krispies treats are sure-fire winners. Don't worry if you're not exactly Wolfgang Puck; if you can read, you can cook. Dig that dusty box of brownie mix out of the pantry (just add eggs and water!) and break out the real mixer. Just don't forget to unplug it before you let her lick the beaters.

- If the several-hundred-dollar "play kitchen" she wants isn't in the budget, you can still play house. Any old table or cabinet can serve as the backdrop for a collection of miniature plates, some pretend appliances, and an assortment of plastic food. *Bon appétit!*

- Her fascination with gizmos won't necessarily be limited to the stereotypically feminine stuff. Get her some scaled-down play tools (great for building fine motor skills), and you may have a puttering partner out in the garage sooner rather than later.

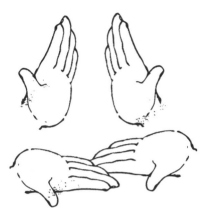

Talk to the Hand

Just because you've mastered pat-a-cake, don't think you're out of the woods. Little girls *adore* clapping games—and they get more challenging as the years progress. From silly nonsense verses to elaborate, multi-stanza rhyming songs, she'll go slap-happy for these digital ditties. When you think you can't possibly muster any more enthusiasm for yet another rousing round, remember that such games help her hone her coordination, memory, and communication skills. (Yours, too!)

Although you can get fancy if you are so inclined, the basic move is simple: Sit across from each other and begin by clapping your (own) hands together at the same time, then reach out with your right hand to clap your daughter's right hand. Next, clap your (own) hands again, and reach out with your left hand to clap her left hand. Repeat indefinitely, trying to establish and maintain some sort of "beat." (Good luck with that!) Here, a handful of verses you'll want to get familiar with:

Say, Say, Oh Playmate
Say, say, oh playmate
Come out and play with me.
And bring out your dollies three,
Climb up my apple tree.
Slide down my rain barrel
Into my cellar door.
And we'll be jolly friends
Forevermore, one, two, three, four!

Say, say, oh playmate,
I cannot play today.
My dollies have the flu,
Boo hoo hoo hoo hoo hoo.
Don't have a rain barrel,
Dad locked the cellar door.
But we'll be jolly friends
Forevermore, one, two, three, four!

Miss Mary Mack
Miss Mary Mack, Mack, Mack
All dressed in black, black, black
With silver buttons, buttons, buttons
All down her back, back, back
She asked her mother, mother, mother
For fifty cents, cents, cents
To see the elephants, elephants, elephants
Jump over the fence, fence, fence
They jumped so high, high, high
They touched the sky, sky, sky
And didn't come back, back, back
Til the fourth of July, ly, ly

About the Author

Jenna McCarthy is an internationally published writer and the author of *The Parent Trip: From High Heels and Parties to Highchairs and Pot-ties, and Cheers to the New Mom/Cheers to the New Dad!* Her work has appeared in more than 50 magazines, on dozens of Web sites, and in several anthologies, including the popular Chicken Soup series. Jenna currently is hard at work on her next project, a practical guide to living with and continuing to love the TV-addicted, listening-impaired, not-quite-handy man that you married. In her spare time, she wonders what she used to do with all of her spare time. Visit her online at www.jennamccarthy.com.

photo by Renée Vernon